His Song
The Cricket Story

VIVIAN COATS
AUTHOR/ILLUSTRATOR OF

IN HIS LOVE, SAFE IN HIS LOVE, HIS SPECIAL LOVE
HIS STAR and HIS PERFECT WAY

HIS SONG
The Cricket Story

Written and Illustrated by

Vivian Coats

authorHOUSE®

AuthorHouse™
1663 Liberty Drive
Bloomington, IN 47403
www.authorhouse.com
Phone: 833-262-8899

Because of the dynamic nature of the Internet, any web
addresses or links contained in this book may have changed
since publication and may no longer be valid. The views
expressed in this work are solely those of the author and do
not necessarily reflect the views of the publisher, and the
publisher hereby disclaims any responsibility for them.

"Scripture taken from the HOLY BIBLE,
NEW INTERNATIONAL VERSION
Copyright 1973, 1978,1984 International
Bible Society.
Used by permission of Zondervan
Bible Publishers."

Scripture marked KJV is taken from
the King James Version of the Bible.

This book is printed on acid-free paper.

ISBN: 978-1-4685-8697-8 (sc)
ISBN: 978-1-4772-2463-2 (e)

Print information available on the last page.

Published by AuthorHouse 06/03/2021

ACKNOWLEDGEMENTS

The author gratefully acknowledges the loved ones that continue to believe and work so diligently on these books:

Jim, my beloved husband, who continues to say, "You can!"

My daughter Jamie Aylstock and my sister Diane Arthurton who are still editing...six books later!

Our dear friends Fred, web technician, and his beautiful wife Linda Aylstock, who continues to pray faithfully for these books.

Roger and Sheila Bouchard, missionaries to America and beyond!

Our beloved pastors, Susan and Jerry Williams, who are not afraid to preach the Word of God in truth.

Ashley Rufo, owner of Ashley's Images Photography (back cover).

And a multitude of people that gave an encouraging word, financial support and/or a prayer in due season---you know who you are!

A generous thank-you to all!!!

Smile! Miracles really do happen every single day!

Joyfully In His Love,
Vivian Coats
Author/Illustrator for Him!

Other Books by
Vivian Coats

In His Love

Safe In His Love

His Special Love

His Star

His Perfect Way:
The Hermit Crab Story

Daddy told his little crickets, "The cricket has a special love song that is heard all around the world."

There are seven continents.
How many continents can you name?
Africa/Asia/Australia/Antarctica/Europe/South America/North America

Let the sea resound, and all that is in it; let the fields be jubilant, and everything in them!

— I Chronicles 16:32 (NIV)

Mama and Daddy Cricket said to their little ones,
"God's love song is seen and heard everywhere."

The birds sing, bees hum, flowers grow and crickets chirp.
Name some other things that proclaim His Song every day.

"I have come that they may have life, and have it to the full."

— John 10:10b (NIV)

Give thanks to the LORD, for he is good; his love endures forever.

—I Chronicles 16:34 (NIV)

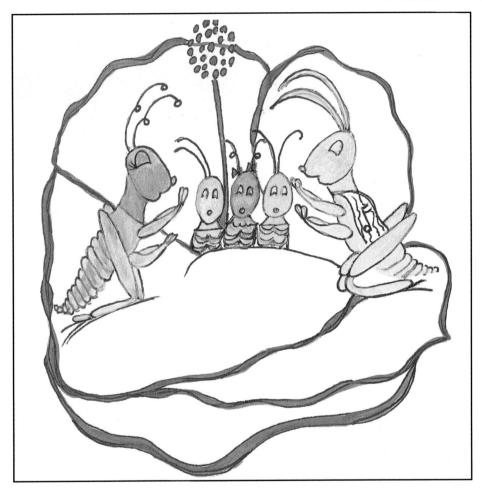

Daddy Cricket declared, "God is always saying, 'I Love You!'"
Everyday we will give Him thanks. Jesus is God's
perfect love song; he taught us how to pray."

*"Our Father which art in heaven, Hallowed be thy name. Thy kingdom
come. Thy will be done in earth, as it is in heaven. Give us this day
our daily bread. And forgive us our debts, as we forgive our debtors.
And lead us not into temptation, but deliver us from evil: For thine
is the kingdom, and the power, and the glory, for ever. Amen."*

—Matthew 6:9-13 (KJV)

As a bridegroom rejoices over his bride, so will your God rejoice over you.
—Isaiah 62:5b (NIV)

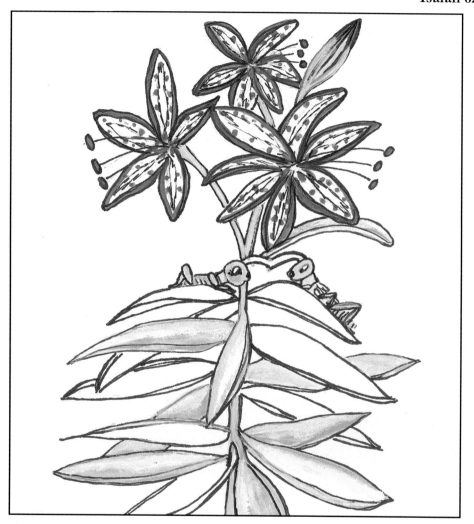

His chirp becomes softer as she comes closer. She touches his antennae so he will know her answer is yes. He sings low and sweet and they fall in love. How can you show God you love Him?

"Here I am! I stand at the door and knock. If anyone hears my voice and opens the door, I will come in and eat with him, and he with me. To him who overcomes, I will give the right to sit with me on my throne, just as I overcame and sat down with my Father on his throne. He who has an ear, let him hear..."
—Revelation 3:20-22 (NIV)

Let everything that has breath praise the LORD. Praise the LORD.

—Psalm 150:6 (NIV)

The cricket's chirp is filled with a song of love and good information. Do you know the snowy tree cricket chirps the temperature? You can count the snowy tree cricket's chirps for 15 seconds then add the number 40. Jesus has many good things to teach us.

"If you hold to my teaching, you are really my disciples. Then you will know the truth, and the truth will set you free."

—John 8:31-32 (NIV)

I will praise the LORD, who counsels me; even at night my heart instructs me.
—Psalm 16:7 (NIV)

Television, movies, and song writers love to use the snowy cricket's chirp. It has a wonderful melody. One man said if moonlight could be heard it would sound like this cricket. God's love is always shining down on us!

" 'Love the LORD your God with all your heart and with all your soul and with all your mind.' This is the first and greatest commandment. And the second is like it: 'Love your neighbor as yourself.' All the Law and the Prophets hang on these two commandments."
—Matthew 22:37-40 (NIV)

I praise you because I am fearfully and wonderfully made; your works are wonderful, I know that full well.

—**Psalm 139:14** (NIV)

The cricket molts 8-10 times before it becomes an adult. Do you know Jesus will make you brand new?

"You should not be surprised at my saying, 'You must be born again.' The wind blows wherever it pleases. You hear its sound, but you cannot tell where it comes from or where it is going. So it is with everyone born of the Spirit."

—**John 3:7 & 8** (NIV)

Every ear has heard the cricket's song. Daddy Cricket was the best fiddler in the field. He would rub his wings together and sing out a love song. The little ones perked up their ears. Do you know a cricket's ears are on its front elbows?

"I tell you the truth, whoever hears my word and believes him who sent me has eternal life and will not be condemned; he has crossed over from death to life."

—*John 5:24* (NIV)

Play skillfully, and shout for joy.
—Psalm 33:3b (NIV)

The crickets began to sing. They could sing higher than the highest note on a piano! God loves it when we sing to him!

"You are the light of the world. A city on a hill cannot be hidden. Neither do people light a lamp and put it under a bowl. Instead they put it on its stand, and it gives light to everyone in the house. In the same way, let your light shine before men, that they may see your good deeds and praise your Father in heaven."
—Matthew 5:14-16 (NIV)

The meadows are covered with flocks and the valleys are mantled with grain; they shout for joy and sing.

—Psalm 65:13 (NIV)

The little crickets began to yawn as everything around them sang for joy.

"I am coming soon. I will write on him the name of my God and the name of the city of my God, the new Jerusalem..."

—Revelation 3:11a & 12c (NIV)

...the sounds of joy and gladness, the voices of bride and bridegroom, and the voices of those who bring thank offerings to the house of the LORD, saying, "Give thanks to the LORD Almighty, for the LORD is good; his love endures forever."

—Jeremiah 33:11 (NIV)

The little crickets soon fell asleep as His Song filled the night air.

"Behold, I am coming soon! I am the Alpha and the Omega, the First and the Last, the Beginning and the End. Blessed are those who wash their robes, that they may have the right to the tree of life and may go through the gates into the city."

—**Revelation 22:12a,13,14** (NIV)

Printed in the United States

Printed in the United States
by Baker & Taylor Publisher Services